THE

ADVENT

OF

GLORY

24 DEVOTIONS FOR CHRISTMAS

R.C. SPROUL

The Advent of Glory
© The R.C. Sproul Credit Shelter Trust, 2023

Published by:
The Good Book Company

thegoodbook.com | thegoodbook.co.uk
thegoodbook.com.au | thegoodbook.co.nz | thegoodbook.co.in

Published in association with the literary agency of Wolgemuth & Associates.

ISBN: 9781784988913 | JOB-007282 | Printed in Turkey

Cover Design by Faceout Studio | Design and art direction by André Parker

CONTENTS

PUBLISHER'S NOTE

Dr R.C. Sproul was a theologian, Presbyterian pastor, and much-loved Bible teacher, whose many books include *The Holiness of God* and *Essential Truths of the Christian Faith*. He died in 2017.

The devotions in this book have been edited with the help of his wife, Vesta Sproul, largely from the transcripts of two series of talks given by Dr Sproul in his lifetime (*The Messiah is Born* and *The Coming of the Messiah*). Each chapter takes one key word from the Christmas story and uses it to meditate on the advent of Christ.

At the end of every chapter you will find a prayer reflecting on what you have just read. You can find out more about the writers of these prayers at the back of the book.

1. CERTAINTY

Growing up in Pittsburgh, it was a tradition in our home to go to the Christmas Eve service every year. We would assemble outside the church at about a quarter after ten, even though the service started at eleven, because so many people would congregate for that special candlelit event. It was filled with pageantry and great choral music, and at about 13 minutes to twelve, the minister would begin his Christmas Eve homily. Just as the clock reached twelve, in the middle of the sermon, the organist would start to play, and the pastor would stop his sermon in mid-sentence as the chimes began to sound. One... two... three... four... We would all sit there in the pews and count them. And as soon as the twelfth tone had registered, the pastor would smile to the congregation, and he would say, "It's Christmas, and may I be the first on this day to wish you a Merry Christmas."

It used to send chills up and down my spine. It was the same every year, and as I grew up, I never wanted to miss it—particularly not on those Christmas Eves when it had snowed and the lawn was covered in the newly fallen snow. There was just something about it; I loved it. But I was not a believer. To me, this was all just exciting pageantry, leading up to the next morning when we got to open the presents.

In September 1957, I had my conversion to Christianity. Like any new Christian, I was absolutely absorbed with the discovery of Christ. It was utter sweetness to me.

I remember my first Christmas as a Christian: coming back home from college for the holidays, driving through the snow to the church, going into the sanctuary, singing the same hymns that I had sung for so many years, hearing the sermon, hearing the chimes strike midnight. And this time, when the minister interrupted his sermon, listened to the chimes, and then leaned over the pulpit and said, "It's Christmas," I was about ready to walk into heaven! It was all the joy that I could handle. Now, for the first time, I was experiencing this pageantry as reality, as truth, as something that had actually taken place.

I was experiencing what Luke would have wanted me to experience when he wrote down the story in the first place.

"It seemed good to me also, having followed
all things closely for some time past, to write
an orderly account for you, most excellent
Theophilus, that you may have certainty
concerning the things you have been taught."

(Luke 1:3-4)

Luke begins his gospel account by stating his purpose. *I
don't want you to just be entertained by this story,* he says;
*I want you to know it with full assurance that these things
that I am about to relate to you are the sober truth.* The accounts that he is going to give to us are not the accounts
of speculation; he has compiled a series of eyewitness
reports (v 1-2).

Luke wasn't an eyewitness himself. He was converted by
the apostles and came under the tutelage of Paul. Much
of what Luke knew, he had gained from his association
with Paul, as well as with others who were among the first
disciples. It's very likely that Luke had the privilege of interviewing Mary, the mother of Christ. He gives us more
information about the birth of Jesus than anybody else,
and he got all that information from an eyewitness.

Luke wrote an orderly, historical, carefully document-
ed account to strengthen our faith and give us certainty.
That was his burden. That was his passion. That was his
task under God: to set forth for us, and for our certainty, how it really was.

So much of Christmas, for so many people, can be just empty excitement and pageantry. But Luke wants to let us know that here, we're not talking about fables or legends or religious fairy tales. Christmas is about something that really took place in space and time. Which—as I discovered that Christmas in 1957—makes it not less wondrous but even more so.

Why can certainty about Christ's life and work lead to joy? Does it for you?

A PRAYER FOR TODAY

by Chris Larson

Our Father and our God, there is none like you.
You are a God who remembers your people as a
tender father remembers his child. The eternal
Word became flesh and dwelt among us, leaving
glory, entering into our fallen world, all to seek
and save that which was lost. We thank you for
your mercy in loving your people to the uttermost.
Nothing is too difficult for you, for with you all
things are possible. And so we know that you
have come near to us in your Son, Jesus Christ,
coming down so that we can be raised up through
faith alone by the power of the Spirit. What
mystery is now revealed. What a gift of love is now
unwrapped for the world to see. May we live with
certainty because of the first advent of our Lord,
even as we await his promised return. Thank you,
our faithful God.

Amen.

2. TIME

The birth of Jesus is the moment that divides history, and I don't just mean into BC and AD. Long before anyone invented that system of counting the years, this was the most important moment in the world—the most important time there has ever been. In Luke's Gospel, we see the first hint of this in the angel's words to Zechariah:

> "Behold, you will be silent and unable to speak
> until the day that these things take place,
> because you did not believe my words, which
> will be fulfilled *in their time.*"
>
> (Luke 1:20, emphasis added)

In the Greek language there are two distinct words for "time." One is *chronos,* and the other is *kairos.* There's enormous significance in the distinction between those two words.

We're familiar with the word *chronos*. We have news-papers called "Chronicle," which tell us about what's happening in our times. We sometimes use the tech-nical word "chronometer" to refer to clocks and time-pieces—things that measure time. The word *chronos*, then, means the normal passing of time. It's how we measure our lives. We have a chronology to what we do: everything that happens is taking place within the con-text of *chronos*.

The word *kairos* is a little tougher to get hold of. It refers to a specific, particular moment in time—a moment of extraordinary significance. It's not that it takes place outside time—it is part of the broad flow of time. But it is a point that defines the meaning of all time.

The distinction between the two is similar to the dis-tinction we make between the words "historical" and "historic." Everything that ever happened is historical, isn't it? But we don't use the term "historic" to refer to every event that ever took place. No, we say that 1066 was historic because of the Battle of Hastings. Or 1776 was historic because of the United States' Declaration of Independence—and so on. The word "historic" is telling us that a certain event is crucial—it has a signifi-cance beyond the normal. It's the same with *kairos*.

This is the word that the angel used when he spoke to Zechariah. "My words ... will be fulfilled in their time."

"Time" there is *kairos*. It speaks of a particular time—a time that was finally coming to pass after centuries and centuries of prophetic promise and of patient waiting by the people of God.

The angel was speaking about the birth of John the Baptist, but John's birth was intended to prepare the way for an even more important moment in time. "When the fullness of time had come," Galatians 4:4 tells us, "God sent forth his Son."

That's a strange image, isn't it—the fullness of time? The word "fullness" is the Greek word *pleroma*, and it means being filled to capacity or filled to the point of bursting. Imagine you've put an empty glass in the sink underneath the spigot. You turn on the water, watch it fill the glass, and leave the tap on. The water continues to stream, and once it reaches the edge of the glass, it begins to spill out. That's *pleroma*: something that is full to the point of overflowing or full to the bursting point.

That's what happened at the moment of Jesus' birth. The time was full.

Our Creator made the world, and from that moment, the clock started to tick. History began, not as an aimless, purposeless flow of time but as something moving forward, moment by moment, second by second, day by day, year by year, toward an appointed destiny. Time passed, and it was being filled up by the plan of God and by the work of God. Then there came that critical juncture in human history when the time—the *kairos*—was filled to capacity at last and burst out with the birth of a baby who was the incarnation of God.

Jesus' birth—in fact, Jesus' whole life, and especially his death and resurrection—these are the crucial moments of *kairos*. These are the moments that define all other moments in history, before or since.

How can you let the moment of Jesus' birth define the moments of your day today?

A PRAYER FOR TODAY

by Rosemary Jensen

*Dear Lord, our sovereign God, you chose the day
that we now call the first Christmas Day before
the foundation of the world. You knew how many
hours each of your children would have to use for
your glory. Forgive me for wasting so much time
in the past year and for not using all my hours in
ways that honored you. Please help me use these
days before Christmas to honor you by preparing
for your return, even as I prepare to celebrate
your birth. I thank you for my birth too, and for
my second birth, which took place by your grace
through faith in you. For Christmas morning,
I pray that my greatest joy will be to wake up
knowing that you were born in time and space as
the God-man—for me and for others who believe
in you as Lord and Savior.*

In your name, amen.

3. IMPOSSIBLE

I don't know how many people I've met in my life-time who say to me that they believe in the deity of Christ, they believe in the resurrection of Christ, and they believe in the atonement of Christ, but they just can't get past the biblical affirmation of the virgin birth of Christ. How could Jesus have been born of a virgin? "It's just impossible," they say.

The virgin birth would have been impossible if there were no God. But God exists, and he can intervene in his creation to do what is ordinarily impossible. The accounts of both Matthew and Luke emphasize that very fact.

> "Now the birth of Jesus Christ took place in
> this way. When his mother Mary had been
> betrothed to Joseph, before they came together
> she was found to be with child."
>
> (Matthew 1:18)

There's no question about what that phrase "they came together" means. Joseph and Mary were betrothed but not yet married. "Before they came together" means "before they had united sexually." And it was prior to that event that Mary was found to be pregnant.

What was the inference that Joseph drew from that? He came to the same conclusion that you and I would. He did not leap to any conclusions that this thing was caused through a virgin conception. No, he assumed that Mary must have slept with somebody else. He knew that she hadn't slept with him, so there had to have been some kind of sexual liaison.

Joseph's next step is no surprise. He didn't want to embarrass her, but he didn't want to marry her if she'd slept with someone else. He decided to divorce her quietly (v 19). But Joseph had jumped to the wrong conclusion because he didn't yet know the crucial truth that we're told at the end of verse 18. Mary "was found to be with child *from the Holy Spirit*" (emphasis added). No sexual liaison but a miracle.

A miracle achieved by the Holy Spirit. Matthew doesn't want us to miss this—so we hear it again when the angel of the Lord appears to Joseph.

> "Joseph, son of David, do not fear to take Mary
> as your wife, for that which is conceived in her
> is from the Holy Spirit." (v 20)

This pregnancy is of God. It is God the Holy Spirit who has brought this seemingly impossible thing, this completely unexpected miracle, to pass.

Meanwhile, in Luke's Gospel, we have the record of the angel Gabriel's announcement of the future birth of Christ to Mary: "Behold, you will conceive in your womb and bear a son, and you shall call his name Jesus" (Luke 1:31). As with Joseph, Mary's response highlights the very thing that so many others since her have found it so difficult to believe: "How will this be, since I am a virgin?" (v 34).

So the angel explains it to her—and Luke, like Matthew, wants to make sure we get the point. "The Holy Spirit will come upon you, and the power of the Most High will overshadow you; therefore the child to be born will be called holy—the Son of God."

When he says that the Spirit will overshadow Mary, the angel is using almost the same language as Genesis 1:2, which tells us that before creation, the Spirit hovered over the waters. *Mary,* the angel is saying, *this is no ordinary son. This son comes by the Spirit. This son comes by the power of God, who created the world. This is the Son of God himself. Do you understand this, Mary?*

He concludes in verse 37 with these words: "Nothing will be impossible with God."

A virgin birth was an impossibility according to the laws of nature. Yet the impossible was made possible by the power of God the Holy Spirit—the same Spirit who came over the waters when God spoke the words that led to the miracle of creation.

God had brought the whole world forth into life, and now he was going to bring forth a baby.

Mary believed it. "Let it be to me according to your word," she said. In saying so, she expressed the faith that God asks from every Christian.

What do you believe God can do? How will you put your faith into action today?

A PRAYER FOR TODAY

by Tim Challies

Our Father in heaven, we thank you that what is impossible for us is possible for you. We thank you that as the one who created all things, you are not beholden to the laws of nature that govern us. We thank you that you are the God who can and who does work miracles. And we thank you especially that you worked the miracle of the birth of your Son. We are so grateful that the almighty and eternal Son of God was conceived by the Spirit and born of a virgin, so that he would be unaffected by the sin that would otherwise have been his inheritance, as it has been ours. Thank you that in sending your Son in his perfect moral purity, he is perfectly suited to be our perfect Savior.

Amen.

4. VIRGIN

Here's another thing to realize about the Christmas story. A virgin birth has happened only once in the whole of history—and yet it wasn't an isolated incident. It was part of what God has been doing since the beginning of time.

To demonstrate this, Matthew points to a specific Old Testament prophecy.

> "All this took place to fulfill what the Lord had spoken by the prophet: 'Behold, the virgin shall conceive and bear a son, and they shall call his name Immanuel' (which means, God with us)." (Matthew 1:22-23)

Matthew is quoting Isaiah 7:14. But he is doing so in a way that doesn't appear to be entirely straightforward. There are several controversies that focus on this text.

The first question is: when Isaiah announced the word of God that a virgin would conceive and bear a child, who was he referring to specifically? Some scholars have pointed out that in the immediate context of Isaiah 7, the reference seems to be to a child that would be born *soon*. It was a time of crisis in Old Testament history, and the birth of this boy would be a sign of what God was going to do among his people (see verses 10, 16-17).

So how could Matthew be right to state that this text was in fact fulfilled much later on in history with the birth of Jesus?

The arguments about this get very complicated and lengthy. But let me try to make things simple with a couple of alternatives.

One is that Isaiah's text, written under the inspiration of the Holy Spirit, had specific reference to one birth and one birth only: namely, the future birth of Jesus of Nazareth, exactly as Matthew indicates.

The other alternative is that there was both a primary and a secondary fulfillment. There was an immediate fulfillment, a sort of down payment of a fulfillment: a boy born straight away, as a sign of what God was about to do. But the most important fulfillment followed centuries later. It's quite possible that this passage in Isaiah did have reference to two time frames: Isaiah's time and Jesus' time.

To understand how this prophecy that "the virgin shall conceive" could have these two fulfillments, we need to know about the second debate surrounding this verse.

It's called the *alma / bethula* controversy. The focus here is on some of the specifics of the Hebrew language. In Hebrew, the term *bethula* means specifically a "virgin": one who is, clinically speaking, free of any history of sexual intercourse. It is the specific, technical term for a virgin. The term *alma*—which is the word Isaiah uses—can be interpreted by the phrase "young woman," and as such does not carry the necessary implication of virginity. So, some have claimed that all Isaiah meant was that someday a young woman would bear a child: not a virgin, just a young woman.

However, the truth is that the phrase "young woman" doesn't quite capture the thrust of this word in Hebrew. In historical English, the term "maiden" did not have the same technical, specific force as the word "virgin," but neither did it have no connotations about the woman's sexual experience at all. It wasn't explicitly drawing attention to the woman's virginity, but it *did* strongly suggest that she was a virgin. It just wasn't the technical term. Similarly, scholars have argued that although the Hebrew word *alma* doesn't necessarily mean "virgin," it certainly carries that implication. "Virgin" *is* therefore a good translation for this word in Isaiah.

In the end, it all comes down to one thing: as believers we come to the Scriptures with an attitude of trust. We believe that the New Testament is trustworthy; and there is no question that the New Testament is claiming far more about the birth of Jesus than that he was born to a young woman. There clearly is the claim that the birth of Christ took place miraculously, supernaturally.

This virgin birth was the beginning of what God was going to do in Christ's incarnation. He had brought life to a virgin's womb; now he would keep on doing the seemingly impossible through the life, death, and resurrection of his Son. The virgin birth was a sign of much, much more.

Which of God's promises—fulfilled or yet to be fulfilled—do you rest on today?

A PRAYER FOR TODAY

by Steven J. Lawson

*God, we praise you that you are majestically
transcendent and perfectly holy. We stand in awe
of your flawless character and impeccable purity.
Your word causes us to marvel at your all-wise
plan to send your Son into this world to be born
of a virgin. We stand amazed that Jesus became
like us, entering the human race, yet unlike us,
being without sin. As we consider his virgin birth,
it causes us again to confess our sinfulness and
our need to pursue personal holiness. We worship
you, for you have clothed us with the perfect
righteousness of Christ so that we may stand
faultless before your throne of grace. Thank you
that you gave your Son, your only Son, to enter
this sin-plagued world to die for our sins. We have
no basis to approach you apart from him. Cause
our hearts to be renewed with devotion for our
holy Savior, who humbled himself and came down
to sinners like us.*

We pray this in Jesus' name. Amen.

5. FAVOR

The first job I ever had was in a shoe repair shop. My boss was a huge bear of a man whom everybody called Uncle Ned. I worked for him as a shoeshine boy, helping with menial tasks.

Every night in that shoe repair shop, it was Ned's tradition to listen to a program called *The Catholic Hour* on the radio. I got so that I could shine shoes in rhythm to the prayers, as we would listen night after night. I remember the Hail Mary in particular. It would start off with the words, "Hail, Mary, full of grace. Blessed are thou amongst women. Blessed is the fruit of thy womb, Jesus." And then we would hear, "Holy Mary, mother of God, pray for us sinners now and at the hour of our death. Amen."

It wasn't until years later, when I read the Scriptures for the first time, that I understood that much of the language of that prayer had been taken directly from the New Testament. The recitation of the Hail Mary dates from the earliest times in Christian history—except for the addition of the part that asks Mary to pray for sinners. That was not added until the 15th century.

The beginning of the prayer is taken from Luke's account of the greeting of the angel Gabriel to Mary. The word "hail" is not a statement of adoration or worship or anything like that—it's simply the old Roman form of greeting. It's like saying, "Hello, Mary." Gabriel said, "Greetings, O favored one" (Luke 1:28). It's this phrase that is translated as "Hail, Mary, full of grace" in the Roman Catholic prayer.

In other words, Roman Catholicism says that the angel is recognizing in Mary someone who is filled with such grace (another word for favor) that she can be a vessel of grace to other people. Mary, it is claimed, is the mother of grace, bestowing favor upon others. But the Protestant interpretation of the text—and I believe the correct one—understands it this way: that Mary isn't the mother of grace but the daughter of grace. She does not bestow favor; she only receives it.

Mary, among all women who have ever lived, was selected to be the mother of Christ—but not because she had earned it. It was not a matter of merit but a matter of grace that Mary received the favor of God. That's why Gabriel adds, "The Lord is with you": it all comes from

God. Some manuscripts—incorporated by many translations although not the ESV—also included "Blessed
are you among women!"

In Jewish families, one of the bleakest things that
could occur to a woman was that she would be child-
less or "barren." Think of the anguish of Elizabeth
when she was unable to conceive, or of Sarah in the
Old Testament, who also had to deal with barrenness
until God, in his mercy, gave her a son. Today, we
don't have the same esteem for the bearing of children.
Modern Western societies sanction abortions by the
millions, turning a jaundiced eye towards the sanctity
of life. Yet even in our jaded culture, there are countless women who still see having a child as among the
highest treasures of blessedness they can enjoy.

But no woman, save one, has ever been so blessed as to
be given the privilege and honor of bearing the Son of
God, and Gabriel appropriately says to Mary, "Blessed
are you among women."

You are highly favored. You are blessed among women.
What can this possibly mean? Mary is frightened (v 29).
But Gabriel says to her, "Do not be afraid, Mary" (v 30).
And he tells her again, "You have found favor with God."

He has not come to bring the judgment of God. He
hasn't come to announce bad tidings. He hasn't visited
with an oracle of doom from on high. No, the angel
brings good news. News of favor undeserved—not

only to Mary but to all of God's people. News of grace.
News that, even though we are sinners, God is with us
and for us.

*How has God shown you favor? In what ways do you
need his favor today?*

A PRAYER FOR TODAY

by Joni Eareckson Tada

O Jesus, if it weren't for your gracious favor toward me, I would be burnt toast. I would be snuffed out in a nanosecond. My sins have earned me a fate worse than death—a ghoulish, hellish existence in a far-flung corner of outer darkness, isolated and in anguish. It's what I deserve. Oh, but just look at you and your mercy! O mercy, how is it that you, the Father, and the Holy Spirit all agreed to rescue me from myself? There's nothing I've done to earn such forgiveness, but in return for your favor, I can—and I will—live a life needing you and thanking you. This Christmas, help me share my redemption story with my relatives, friends, and neighbors who have yet to know your favor. This season, may the same gospel that saved me also save those for whom I pray right now.

In Jesus' name, amen.

6. MOTHER

In the first few centuries of the church, there were several occasions on which leaders from across the church gathered to debate and affirm their precise understanding of some of the essential truths of Christianity.

In 431, they met in Ephesus, in modern-day Turkey. The topic up for debate was what Christians should call Mary. Should it be *Theotokos*, "mother of God"? Or was that overstating Mary's role? Was it safer just to say *Christotokos*, "mother of Christ"?

Some Christians today might still shrink back in horror at the suggestion that Mary could be regarded as *Theotokos*, "mother of God." After all, God is eternal, and he doesn't have a mother.

However, in Ephesus, the church affirmed that title, asserting that it was right to refer to Mary as the mother of God.

We, too, must embrace this truth. This title is important because it means that Mary was the woman who bore the Son of God incarnate. No one is claiming that Jesus' divine nature came from Mary or that the Son of God didn't exist before Mary bore him. "Mother of God" simply means that Mary bore Jesus Christ—the one divine person who is the Son of God incarnate. In other words, Christ is not a human person and a divine person. He is a divine person in whom are perfectly united a human nature and a divine nature, "without confusion, without change, without division, without separation," as the Council of Chalcedon (in 451) puts it.

Mary was indeed the mother of the one who was God incarnate. She had a sacred responsibility that no other mother in human history ever had: she reared a child who was Immanuel—who was God himself.

Mary was already troubled when she heard the angel's initial message of favor. When she heard that her child would be "the Son of the Most High," her distress can only have increased. "How will this be?" (Luke 1:34). *Me, bearing in my womb the Messiah? Me, giving birth to the Lord himself?*

When God passed by Moses on the mountain, he told Moses that he could not see his face and live (Exodus 33:20). When a certain Israelite placed his hand for just a moment on the ark of the covenant—the symbol of God's presence—he was struck dead (2 Samuel 6:6-7).

But now God had come to earth as a touchable, visible, vulnerable child. Truly human, truly God, Jesus was born to Mary as the divine Son. When Mary and Joseph looked into the face of Mary's firstborn child, they were looking into the face of God.

Mary was a human—ordinary—just like you and me. And yet she was also the mother of God, thanks only to his immense grace.

It is a mystery that we will not fully understand but which we must embrace—as Mary did. Ultimately, she surrendered to the messenger. "Let it be to me according to your word" (v 38). Not everything could have made sense to Mary at that moment; yet even in what she did not understand, she was willing to obey.

We can best honor Mary today by following her example of willing submission and obedience to the will of God, even when we don't fully understand how he is working out his purposes in history. He will never ask you or me to agree to such a task as Mary's, but in her obedience and her acceptance of God's plans, we see a noteworthy model for every human being: for every man and woman, every mother and father.

What truths about God or commandments of God do you struggle with? How can you trust him in your confusion?

A PRAYER FOR TODAY

by Sinclair B. Ferguson

Lord Jesus Christ, Son of God and son of Mary, I marvel at the sheer wonder of who you really are. You are truly God, and yet for our sake you also became truly human. It is beyond me to understand this! And yet, Lord Jesus, in the blinding light of your glorious person, everything else becomes clearer. Thank you for taking our human nature, living our life, dying our death, and becoming our Saviour. Heavenly Father, how can we ever thank you enough for planning to redeem us from our sin and guilt? How can we ever thank you, Holy Spirit, for superintending the conception and birth and the saving life and death of our Lord Jesus? With a full heart I praise you, Father, Son, and Holy Spirit. Bring me, like Mary, to yield my life to you in the obedience of faith.

Answer my prayer, Lord, for your glory. Amen.

7. PROMISE

"Blessed is she who believed that there would be
a fulfillment of what was spoken to her from
the Lord." (Luke 1:45)

To prepare us to consider those words, spoken by
Elizabeth to Mary when the two women met during the course of their pregnancies, I want to take you first to some words Paul wrote to the Roman believers. The first verses of Paul's letter to the Romans are rarely, if ever, considered to be part of the Christmas message. But when we look at them, we will quickly and clearly see why they are significant for Christmas.

"Paul, a servant of Christ Jesus, called to be an
apostle, set apart for the gospel of God, which
he promised beforehand through his prophets
in the holy Scriptures, concerning his Son…"
(Romans 1:1-3)

Paul begins with his normal identification of himself as a slave bound to Christ and as an apostle, who has been commissioned by Christ to represent the teaching of Christ to the church. But he also speaks of his being called for a particular mission. His task is to proclaim "the gospel of God."

Paul does not just mean that he is about to declare good news about God. The grammatical form of the phrase "the gospel of God" indicates possession: that is to say, we could rewrite these words to say that Paul is set apart and called to preach "God's gospel." The gospel is something that is God's possession; it comes from God. The point is that this is not Paul's gospel. This is not the church's gospel. This is not invented by human beings. It is God's message, God's announcement, God's good news, and it was now being entrusted to the apostles—men specially commissioned by the Lord Jesus Christ—who were set apart by God to proclaim it.

This gospel that comes to us from God is a gospel that God "promised beforehand." Often, when the New Testament writers refer to some aspect of the work of Jesus, they say that it happened *according to the Scriptures*. At the very outset of the proclamation of the gospel, we see that the advent of Christ was also *according to the Scriptures*. When Paul talks about the coming of Christ, he's talking not about something that exploded onto the scene of history suddenly and unexpectedly but about something that God had promised centuries and centuries before.

The reason why we call this season Advent is because Advent means "a coming to" in Latin. We are celebrating the coming of Christ into the world at Bethlehem—a long-expected, long-awaited coming, "promised beforehand ... in the Scriptures."

That's important for us who live now, after the first advent of Jesus, because we too are waiting. We're looking ahead to the future, to the return of Jesus, which is often called his second advent.

A feeling that people frequently experience is doubt. "Well, we've been waiting for 2,000 years, and Christ has not yet returned. Maybe it's a myth. Maybe he's not coming." This is exactly the attitude of doubt and discouragement that many people in the 1st century felt with respect to the *first* advent. They knew the Scriptures. They knew that centuries before, the prophets had predicted that the Messiah would come. Generation after generation waited eagerly and expectantly, looking for the coming of the Messiah, but he didn't come. After a while some people began to say, *Well, he's never coming.* Paul says, however, that the gospel he proclaims is the very thing that God himself had promised through the prophets.

Have you ever experienced a sense of doubt or frustration about the promises of God? Many times God seems to work so slowly that we begin to despair. Will he ever perform the promises that he has made? This is the context in which to read the words that Elizabeth said of Mary:

> "Blessed is she who believed that there would be a fulfillment of what was spoken to her from the Lord." (Luke 1:45)

Blessed is she, and blessed will you and I be, also. The true people of God in the Old Testament were those who were willing to wait for the advent of their Messiah. Even as today we look back at the fulfillment of those promises, we still stand waiting for the final advent of Christ. Let us wait with devotion to the gospel God gave us and with confidence in the trustworthiness of God's promises.

Where do you need confidence in God today?

A PRAYER FOR TODAY

by Chris Larson

*Our Father and our God, holy is your name,
and may your name be seen as holy in all the
earth. The promise given to Abraham, that in
his offspring the nations would be blessed, you
have kept. You are a promise-keeping God, and
so we know that the good news of Jesus Christ is
the fulfillment of promises acknowledged by your
people through the ages. With thankful hearts,
we look back at Jesus Christ coming into the
world. With trusting hearts, we wait with patient
eagerness for the redemption of all things. How
long, O Lord, until you come again? We love you,
and we long to look on our Savior, who has loved
us so faithfully, and to be in the presence of Father,
Son, and Spirit, proclaiming your holy name in
the new heavens and the new earth.*

Amen.

8. REDEEMED

> "Blessed be the Lord God of Israel, for he has
> visited and redeemed his people ... as he spoke
> by the mouth of his holy prophets from of old."
>
> (Luke 1:68, 70)

Those are the words spoken by Zechariah as he came to grapple with what these miraculous births—of his own son, John, and of Mary's son, Jesus—were going to mean. Jesus had not yet drawn breath, but Zechariah, filled with the Holy Spirit, saw the truth. Redemption was coming—just as it was promised of old.

The promises start right from the beginning, in Genesis 3:15, where God tells the serpent:

> "I will put enmity between you and the woman,
>   and between your offspring and her
>   offspring;

> he shall bruise your head,
>> and you shall bruise his heel."

It might surprise you that this promise is sometimes called the "first gospel." The good news is not about warfare or conflict or enmity. The good news is about peace, about the cessation of warfare, about the end to hostility. Yet this is a promise of enmity. This so-called first gospel is given in the context not of a promise of blessing but of a divine curse.

Throughout the Old Testament, there is an acute awareness that the world is fallen: it has come under the curse of God because of sin. God curses Eve with pain in childbirth, and he curses Adam with difficult labor as he tries to survive, to till and cultivate the earth (v 16-19). Instead of the earth gladly and willingly bringing forth its fruit, it resists, putting forth thorns and briars and weeds and droughts and floods and all of those problems that we have in eking out survival as human beings. We're told that the whole creation groans, as if it's in the pangs of labor (Romans 8:22). The whole of creation is under a curse as a result of sin.

The first promise of enmity that God makes is part of this curse. Enmity will exist between the woman and the serpent. In other words, Satan is humanity's mortal enemy. Being in a fallen world means battling against the devil's temptations and accusations.

But God doesn't stop there. He also looks to the future. The word translated "offspring" in Genesis 3:15 is actually "seed" or "descendant," and if you look carefully at the grammar, you see that the promise ultimately looks ahead to one specific descendant. There was one coming who would be born of a woman and who would be the greatest enemy the serpent would ever have. That is Christ.

This promise of enmity isn't bad news, then—or rather, it's bad news for the serpent, but it's good news for us. God has established enmity between Satan and Christ. There is someone on our side. There is a battle to be waged on our behalf.

The curse continues: "He shall bruise your head, and you shall bruise his heel." So the promise is that the one who is coming, born of a woman, is going to crush the head of the serpent—although, in the process of that crushing, the heel of the promised one will be bruised. It's the image of a man killing a snake by stomping on its head with his foot, but getting his heel bruised as he does so. This has been seen for centuries as an image of the atonement—an image of the cross. In the drama of the cross, we see the crushing blow that Christ, the descendant of Eve, delivered to Satan. We see that he did it at great expense. He did not do it without injury and pain to himself, but, ultimately, he is the victor.

From the earliest pages of the Old Testament, a promise has been made for the future about one who will come to crush the head of evil and to bring about re-demption for God's people.

There were many centuries to come, more promises to be made, more pain to endure. The world was cursed. It still is. But if it's groaning in labor pains, it's going to give birth. This is what Zechariah foresaw. Victory has been won, and while we labor under a curse, we also labor in the certain hope of redemption.

What temptations and sins attack you at the moment? Where do you need the help of the serpent-crusher?

A PRAYER FOR TODAY

by Rosemary Jensen

Dear Jesus, my Redeemer, I get so much joy when I sing, "Redeemed, redeemed, redeemed by the blood of the Lamb,"* because you are that Lamb. You are the one who came into the world to redeem me by your blood. So often I fail to thank you for the fact that I am redeemed, not by what I have done but by what you have done for me. Please forgive me for not looking to you for my redemption but instead thinking I have somehow earned my freedom from Satan's power by being a good person. Thank you for not only freeing me from the power of Satan today but for also giving me eternal life. Please help me understand more fully what your coming to earth as a baby, living a perfect life, dying on the cross, and being raised again did for me. I ask you to prompt me to live as you want me to live now in these days before Christmas and to give all the glory to you.

Amen.

* *"Redeemed, How I Love to Proclaim It" by Fanny Crosby*

9. HAPPENED

"In those days a decree went out from Caesar
Augustus that all the world should be
registered. This was the first registration when
Quirinius was governor of Syria. And all went
to be registered, each to his own town."

(Luke 2:1-3)

W e're all familiar with that introduction to the
narrative of the birth of Jesus. In fact it might
be so familiar that the words just slip over us. We race
ahead; we want to get to Bethlehem—but it's worth
pausing over these phrases, which place Christ's birth
concretely in the context of real history.

Curiously, the ESV doesn't translate the first word of the
Greek in these verses: *egeneto*. That word literally means "it
happened." The King James Bible renders it this way:

> "And it came to pass in those days, that there
> went out a decree from Caesar Augustus that
> all the world should be taxed." (v 1)

"It came to pass." That's an important phrase with which to begin the story of Christ's birth.

We all know the classic beginning of fairy tales: "Once upon a time…" We use that particular opening to create a setting that is vague, for a story that is uncertain with respect to any specific time period and even any place. In other words, we know from the beginning that the story never really took place. Luke, however, isn't writing a fairy tale. What he's saying is that something happened—and what happened took place in time and space. Something happened, and he recorded it. Luke has indicated already, in the preface to his Gospel, that he has undertaken his own research as he's written this account—interviewing eyewitnesses and so on (1:1-2). The affirmations that he is making here are affirmations of history.

Most of us take this for granted, but we shouldn't. It's worth comparing it with other faiths and beliefs. For the Greeks, for example, the activities of their gods and god-desses were not related to history. They were mytholog-ical. Do you know the story of the birth of the goddess Athena? Greeks believed that she sprang fully-clothed straight out of the head of her father, Zeus. Athena was never cloaked in the garb of history.

Jesus' birth isn't like that.

It happened that a decree went out from Caesar Augustus. In the next sentence, Luke says that a census took place while Quirinius was governing Syria. The setting for the birth narrative of Jesus is placed squarely in the context of secular history. There was a Caesar Augustus, and there was a Quirinius. There was a city named Rome, and there was a region called Syria. Luke's assertion about the birth of Jesus is that it is no myth or fairy tale. It's set directly in the context of history.

Jesus' birth came to pass, as did the rest of Jesus' life, his death, and his resurrection. In 2 Peter 1:16, Peter makes this comment:

> "For we did not follow cleverly devised myths
> when we made known to you the power and
> coming of our Lord Jesus Christ, but we were
> eyewitnesses of his majesty."

He's talking not about the birth of Jesus, of course, but of the transfiguration: the moment when the majesty of Christ's glory broke through the veil of his humanity and his disciples saw it. But the point remains the same: Peter seeks to establish his readers in the truth (v 12). He says, "I will make every effort so that after my departure you may be able at any time to recall these things" (v 15).

It happened—and this is a crucial point for the Christian community to understand and embrace. Some schools of thought describe a "theology of timelessness," which wrenches the Christian message out of the context of history and reduces Christianity to some kind of existential religious experience. That would leave us without any real basis for our beliefs. It's important to know that it *happened*. Jesus was born, lived, died, and rose again. Those are truths we can be established in. That is history which we can build our lives upon.

What difference will it make to your life today that Jesus' birth, life, death, and resurrection really happened?

A PRAYER FOR TODAY

by Tim Challies

*Father, your word is full of treasures, so we pray
that we would commit ourselves to reading it
carefully and to diligently paying attention to each
chapter, each verse, each word. And we thank
you that the word does not only withstand such
scrutiny but generously rewards it, for as we pay
attention to each detail, our confidence increases.
We see that your word is true, we see that it is
accurate, we see that it is reliable. We see that it
is the only trustworthy guide to tell us who you
are and what you demand of us, the creatures you
created in your image and for your glory. So please,
Lord, enable and equip us to be true and lifelong
students of your inerrant, infallible, sufficient, and
holy word.*

Amen.

10. RULER

The birth of Jesus was a biblical prophecy that would be fulfilled to the letter, but God brought it to pass using a strange set of circumstances. One aspect of this was that he was working one of the most powerful rulers of that time like putty or clay in his hands.

Caesar Augustus, also called Octavian, was the first Roman emperor and the most powerful man ever to rule over the Roman Empire. He ascended to the emperor's seat of authority in 30 BC, and he reigned until he died in AD 14. For 44 years he ruled over Rome, and it was during this period that Rome reached the pinnacle of its power—economically, culturally, and from a military standpoint. The empire stretched from north Africa to northern France, from the coasts of Spain to the deserts of Syria. People living in what are today Algeria, Romania, the Netherlands, and even

Russia knew Augustus' name. Rome was so powerful during the reign of Augustus that, for the most part, the conquered peoples did not challenge his rule. Peace pervaded the Roman Empire. That's why another name for this era is the "Pax Romana," or "peace of Rome"—a peace achieved and maintained by the might of the emperor's armies.

That's one of the great ironies of history: it was during the peace of Rome that the true Prince of Peace was born.

We read in Luke 2:1 that a decree or edict went out from Caesar Augustus that "all the world should be registered." All of these masses and multitudes of people in the conquered territories of Rome were scrambling to reach their birthplaces (or their legal residence, where they might have held property) to register for this census. It came at a most inconvenient time in the lives of Joseph and his pregnant wife. Here she was in the ninth month, and they had to make a 90-mile journey from Nazareth to Bethlehem to register to be taxed.

I found it vexing to go all the way to City Hall to change my driver's license when I moved from Pennsylvania to Florida, and I didn't have to walk 90 miles with a pregnant wife in order to do it. Yet, in the final stages of this pregnancy, these apparently insignificant peasants were forced to make this arduous journey by the decree of the emperor.

But the emperor's decree was really issued by a higher power. It was from Almighty God, who had decreed from before the foundation of the earth that his beloved Son would be born in Bethlehem, the city of David.

Centuries before, God had moved Cyrus, king of another great empire, to allow the Jewish people to return to their own land and rebuild Jerusalem and the temple there. Cyrus was a great man—but God was greater. Through the prophet Isaiah, God said to Cyrus:

> "For the sake of ... Israel my chosen,
>> I summon you by name
>>> and bestow on you a title of honor,
>>> though you do not acknowledge me."
>
> (Isaiah 45:4, NIV)

God had chosen Cyrus, raised him up, and was working through him—all despite the fact that Cyrus himself knew nothing of God.

Augustus didn't either. He had no idea that his decree for this enrollment, this census, had any major significance. It was an administrative necessity. He presumably wasn't thinking about the future of his entire civilization, and certainly not about the history of the world. Yet the biggest reason why people know Caesar Augustus' name is not because of the people he conquered or the peace he achieved or the society he built. People know Augustus' name for this reason above all others:

because it is mentioned in passing in the story of the birth of the King in Bethlehem.

What does it mean to you that God can work through any and all people and circumstances?

A PRAYER FOR TODAY

by Steven J. Lawson

God, we humble ourselves beneath your mighty right hand and confess that you alone are the supreme Ruler over all. Your ways are past finding out. As high as the heavens are above the earth, so are your ways above our ways. We stand amazed that you work inscrutably through both good and evil to accomplish your sovereign purposes here upon the earth. We are astonished that you never need to have the circumstances just right in order to fulfill your plans for history. You raise up one ruler and lower another. Earthly kings fulfill their role, which you gave them. Forgive us for when we lose sight of this, presuming that we are in control of what comes to pass. We bow before your throne, which is high and lifted up above the heavens. We lower ourselves and acknowledge your right to rule every area of our lives. You alone are God, and there is no other.

We pray this in Jesus' name. Amen.

11. BETHLEHEM

The great 20th-century filmmaker Cecil B. DeMille was famed for the epic scale of his productions. His 1952 film *The Greatest Show on Earth*, a drama set in a traveling circus, involved more than 80 real-life circus acts and hundreds of animals, including elephants, monkeys, and big cats—plus a spectacular set piece involving a wrecked train. The movie cost four million dollars (that's about 40 million in today's money) and made far more. No one could have any doubt that DeMille and the film company that backed him were wealthy, clever, and powerful.

But God is not like Cecil B. DeMille. God brings the mighty out of the small.

One of my favorite Old Testament prophecies about the Messiah is found in a somewhat obscure portion of one of the lesser-known minor prophets: Micah 5.

This chapter opens with an announcement of doom and judgment; the land will be attacked and afflicted.

> "Now muster your troops,
>   O daughter of troops;
>   siege is laid against us;
>   with a rod they strike the judge of Israel
>   on the cheek." (Micah 5:1)

One of the functions that the prophets in the Old Testament served was to act as prosecuting attorneys for God. The prophet's task was to serve a court summons to a guilty people who had violated the terms of their covenant—of their contract, if you like—with their God. These prosecutors would call the people to account and then pronounce God's sentence of judgment upon them.

Yet at the same time, when God sent his prophets to pronounce these verdicts of judgment against his people, he would always temper that justice with mercy. There was always a "however"—always a promise of his ultimate work of redemption contained within the threat.

And so, in the midst of this prophecy of judgment, there comes a little breath of fresh air—a brief statement of good news.

> "But you, O Bethlehem Ephrathah,
>   who are too little to be among the clans
>   of Judah,

from you shall come forth for me
  one who is to be ruler in Israel,
whose coming forth is from of old,
    from ancient days.
Therefore he shall give them up until the time
  when she who is in labor has given birth;
then the rest of his brothers shall return
    to the people of Israel.
And he shall stand and shepherd his flock in
  the strength of the Lord,
   in the majesty of the name of the Lord
    his God.
And they shall dwell secure, for now he shall
  be great
   to the ends of the earth.
And he shall be their peace." (v 2-5)

Here are some themes we see very frequently in Old Testament prophecies of the coming Messiah—and which we will see more of in the next few chapters of this book. He is the one who will come as a king, like David. He will rescue his people. He will redeem those who remain faithful to the promises of God. He will bring peace.

But what's special about this particular prophecy is its beginning.

It's astonishing to me that centuries before the birth of Christ, the town that was specifically mentioned as the future birthplace of the Messiah King was a tiny, apparently insignificant village—"too little to be among the clans of Judah."

You would think that the Messiah would have been destined to be born in Jerusalem, at Mount Zion in the Holy City—the place that David had established as the central sanctuary and the capital of the whole nation. Instead, it was in Bethlehem.

Bethlehem is about four and a half miles south of Jerusalem. Even today it is not a big place. You can still see the shepherds herding their sheep in the fields around it. In Micah's time it was even more insignificant, but from it came one who would be great to the very ends of the earth (v 4).

God works like that. There are big, spectacular set pieces sometimes, but, more often, isn't it the little things he chooses? The womb of a girl nobody had ever heard of, the hillside scattered with sheep, the town easily forgotten, a criminal's cross—and my life and your life.

In what ways do you feel little? What difference does it make to know that God is the one who brings the mighty out of the small?

A PRAYER FOR TODAY

by Joni Eareckson Tada

O Jesus, I am astounded that you, the King of the universe, chose to be born in a parking lot behind a Bethlehem motel with a blinking No Vacancy sign. You incarnated yourself inside the frail frame of a poor peasant girl, and you chose an animal shed for her delivery room. You chose to announce your Messiah manifesto to a ragtag group of scruffy shepherds. Oh, this Advent, help me to understand that this is the way you work. You take delight in choosing the unlikely, the unlovely, and the poorly gifted. I marvel at how this turns up the wattage on your glory. So, here at year's end, I commit not to cherish inflated ideas of my own importance but humbly lower myself before your majesty. I lay my Christmas gift at your feet, yielding my weakness for your kingdom purposes.

For your glory and honor, Jesus, amen.

12. DAVID

Prophet after prophet in the Old Testament enlarges on the promise of God of this one who was to come. I don't know exactly how many prophecies there are altogether in the Old Testament about the coming of the Messiah, but some have numbered them in the thousands.

The one who was to come would be like Moses, a prophet raised up by the Lord (Deuteronomy 18:15). The one who was to come would mediate a new covenant for his people (Jeremiah 31:31-34). The one who was to come would be a servant, who would suffer and die for the sins of others (Isaiah 53:1-12).

And the one who was to come would be like David.

"In that day I will raise up
  the booth of David that is fallen
and repair its breaches,

> and raise up its ruins
> and rebuild it as in the days of old."
>
> (Amos 9:11)

David, of course, was the greatest king in all of Israel's history. He extended the borders of Israel and made what had been a tiny little nation, about the size of the state of Maryland, into a regional power. He brought wealth, trade, industry, and so on to the Jewish nation. David distinguished himself as a great statesman and political administrator. He introduced one of the most prosperous economic periods in the nation's history. He was also, as we know, a poet, a musician, and a man after God's own heart.

David inaugurated what has always been seen as the golden age of Israel. But within one generation, during the reign of David's son Solomon, this golden age began to tarnish. By the second generation, it had turned to rust. The kingdom was split into two, with the north ruled by Jeroboam the son of Nebat and the south ruled by Solomon's son Rehoboam. After that, the history of this divided kingdom reads like a rogue's gallery. There was wicked monarch after wicked monarch. Much of what had been glorious about the kingdom of Israel was now fallen and in ruins.

Imagine a little booth—a ramshackle building tilted over on its side with wild vegetation covering it.

Decaying, rotting, mildewing. That's the image of what David's kingdom had become by the time of the prophet Amos. It was a shambles. No wonder that people longed for the restoration of the kingdom of Israel—longed for a kingship that would mirror and reflect the graciousness of the era of David. This is what Amos said God was going to provide. One would come who would raise up that which had fallen and rebuild it as in the days of old. A king like David would reign once more.

In the time of Jesus, many people thought that this Messiah would be a political revolutionary. He would drive the hated Romans out of the land—just as David had defeated the Philistines—and restore the earthly kingdom of Israel. They expected a political deliverer. But Jesus said, "My kingdom is not of this world" (John 18:36).

The battle Jesus won transcended any struggle that takes place in ordinary combat or warfare on this planet. His victory is a victory over cosmic forces: Satan, hell, and death itself. His throne is in the heavenly realms (Hebrews 8:1). His rule is over all things, not just over one nation. Jesus is a king far greater than David.

The angel proclaimed this truth when he instructed Mary regarding how her son would be named:

> "He will be great and will be called the Son of
> the Most High. And the Lord God will give to

him the throne of his father David, and he will
reign over the house of Jacob forever, and of
his kingdom there will be no end."

(Luke 1:32-33)

Jesus was the Son of the Most High God and the Son
of David: the one whom God had promised would be
David's son and David's Lord.

*What does it mean to you that Jesus is ruling from his
heavenly throne right now? What difference does it
make that he will still be ruling tomorrow, and the day
after, and next year, and next century?*

A PRAYER FOR TODAY

by Sinclair B. Ferguson

Gracious Lord Jesus Christ, you are David's greater son, his Lord and mine. From the beginning you have reigned over all things visible and invisible, both in heaven and on earth. You are sovereign over both nature and history. In you the Father's oldest and most difficult-to-keep promises have been fulfilled. I praise you for bending down and lifting us onto your shoulders to take us home to your heavenly glory. Thank you for coming to conquer the dark powers that mar our lives. And thank you, too, that though you were demeaned and rejected by those who would not have you reign over them, all authority in heaven and earth is now yours. I bow before you as my King and pray that when, today, I stand in the presence of others, your reign over me will be obvious to them.

Hear my prayer, O Lord. Amen.

13. KING

Prophet after prophet, image after image told the people what to expect of their coming Messiah; but perhaps no prophecy is more vivid than the one found in Isaiah 9. This very well-known prophecy has become an integral part of the liturgy, the imagery, and the pageantry of Christmas. It tells of a king, one who will rule "on the throne of David" (v 7). It begins:

> "For to us a child is born,
>> to us a son is given;
>> and the government shall be upon his
>> shoulder,
>>> and his name shall be called
>> Wonderful Counselor, Mighty God,
>>> Everlasting Father, Prince of Peace."
>>>>>>> (Isaiah 9:6)

The first two lines tell us that this is a prophecy of the birth of a child. But the rest tells us that this was going to be quite some child. He would be like no other before or since.

It's striking that he is described as a "counselor." That term was usually used in Old Testament times to describe not the king himself but the king's most trusted advisor. But here the king himself is the counselor. He doesn't need an advisor to teach him how to rule in justice and in wisdom because he in himself has wisdom in full measure.

The word "wonderful" here, we need to be aware, does not just mean "very good" or "pleasant" or "desirable." The original meaning of the term is "full of wonder": astonishing, amazing, something that evokes awe. Isaiah is saying that this King who is to come will be a Counselor *par excellence*. He will be a Counselor whose wisdom will amaze and astonish.

This king who is to come will also be called "Mighty God." This is an allusion not simply to God's omnipotence in an abstract sense but to a particular type of situation we see him in throughout the Old Testament. The Mighty God is the God who is invincible in warfare.

Keep in mind that David distinguished himself as a warrior of the highest degree before he ascended to the throne. He was Israel's mighty warrior. A song about him went, "Saul has struck down his thousands, and

David his tens of thousands" (1 Samuel 18:7). It's no surprise then that this king who will be like David will be a mighty warrior—the God who will fight triumphantly for his people. A conquering king. This Mighty God-King would conquer the fiercest enemies of all: Satan, hell, and death itself.

Doesn't it seem strange that this king who will be born is not only a mighty warrior of God but also the "Prince of Peace"? It is not strange at all, as a matter of fact—because the purpose of this king's warfare is to end warfare. He will end conflict and bring peace—peace between the nations and, above all, peace with God (Ephesians 2:14-18).

"Everlasting Father" might also seem to be a strange title to give to a king. We don't generally think of a king as a father. Yet the character of God in his reign over his people is expressed in this image. The king in Israel, when the monarchy was first established, was supposed to rule under God's authority. The king was not to rule over his subjects in order to oppress them, to tyrannize them, or to exploit them for his own purposes. He was to rule over the nation as a father—displaying the love of God as well as the administration of God, and the care and nurture of God alongside the justice of God. "As a father shows compassion to his children, so the LORD shows compassion to those who fear him" (Psalm 103:13).

The adjective that describes this Father is "everlasting." The old kingdom is like a fallen booth—but the new David, the new king, will have a kingdom that will not rust, will not decay, and will not fall away.

All of these things are true of the one whom Mary wrapped in swaddling cloths and laid in a manger. He was a child like no other before or since. And so the Nativity isn't something simply to smile sweetly at or coo over. This child's reign shall be forever. Let's fall on our knees. Let's bow down in awe at the Wonderful Counselor, Mighty God, Everlasting Father, and Prince of Peace.

Which aspect of Jesus' identity do you most need to remember in your life at the moment—Wonderful Counselor, Mighty God, Everlasting Father, or Prince of Peace?

A PRAYER FOR TODAY

by Chris Larson

Our Father and our God, you reign from everlasting to everlasting. You rule over all things, and nothing can successfully oppose you or thwart your plans. As sovereign, you send out your word and accomplish precisely what you have intended. Through the gospel of Jesus Christ and the power of your Spirit, you are bringing light out of darkness as you conquer hearts, transform lives, restore families, renew communities, and subdue the nations. Even now, Lord, you are reigning from heaven. Forgive us when we rebel against your reign. Help us to remember that just as your kingship will never come to an end, your redeeming love will never grow cold.

Hear us, we pray, for the sake of your dear Son and our Savior and King, Jesus Christ. Amen.

14. GOVERNMENT

Do you ever feel like you carry the world on your shoulders? The image comes from a Greek mythological figure named Atlas, who literally bears the world on his back. You'll find statues of him in art galleries and stately homes. He's hunched over, muscles straining, face serious, and on his shoulders sits the entire globe.

We recognize ourselves in that image; we know the strain of carrying responsibilities in our families or at work, or the burden of worry about our nation or our world. Sometimes it's like we bear the world on our shoulders, and we can't see how we can ever be free.

But Isaiah's famous prophecy reminds us whose shoulders the burden of the world is actually on.

> "For to us a child is born,
>   to us a son is given;

and the government shall be upon his
shoulder." (Isaiah 9:6)

In the context of Isaiah's prophecy, this king will be born
for God's chosen people. It's the government of Israel
he'll carry on his shoulders. So this is not simply the
joyful announcement of a particular set of parents, celebrating the impending birth of their baby. This is a child
that is to be born for the nation: "to us."

But Jesus is not simply the king of Israel. He is the
"King of kings" and "Lord of lords" (Revelation 19:16).
This particular word structure means more than that
Jesus has a position of authority by which he rules over
lesser kings. It also indicates the supremacy of Jesus in
his monarchical majesty. He is King in the highest possible sense of kingship—and his realm is all creation.

In Paul's letter to the Philippians, he writes that after
his ascension, Jesus was given the name that is above
all names (Philippians 2:9). The name that he has
been given rises above all other titles that anyone can
receive—because it is a name that is reserved for God.
"Jesus Christ is Lord" (v 11). This is God's title, *Adonai*,
which means "the one who is absolutely sovereign."
Again, this title is one of supreme governorship for the
one who is the King of all of the earth.

The King is already in place. Jesus has already received
all authority on heaven and on earth. That means that at

this very moment, the supreme authority over the kingdoms of this world and over the entire cosmos is in the hands of King Jesus. There is no inch of real estate and no symbol of power in this world that is not under his ownership and his rule at this very moment.

Thus Isaiah goes on:

> "Of the increase of his government and of peace
>   there will be no end,
> on the throne of David and over his kingdom,
>   to establish it and to uphold it
> with justice and with righteousness
>   from this time forth and forevermore."
>
> (Isaiah 9:7)

It's easy to put our hope in earthly governments to bring justice and peace. Politics is in the news every day; it's hard not to think about it. With every fresh election, with every new bill or law, so many people's hopes are established, and so many others' hopes are dashed. But the rule of the world isn't on earthly politicians' shoulders any more than it is on ours.

In this Christmas season, take some time to think about politics in a different way. What the New Testament tells us is that right now, the person who is the chief executive officer in the cosmos—the person who has ascended to the highest political position in the universe—is this child who was born, the Son who was given to us.

We're under local government and we're under national government—but all these governments are ultimately still under the dominion of Christ. Right now, today, wherever we are in the world, we live under a government ruled by Jesus. It's on his shoulders that the whole world rests.

What burdens do you need to give to Jesus today—whether personal, national, or global?

A PRAYER FOR TODAY

by Rosemary Jensen

Dear Lord Jesus, Ruler of heaven and earth, it is comforting to remember today that you carry the burdens of this world on your shoulders. Thank you that I am not responsible for the world, my country, or my community. Forgive me for worrying about what politicians, military leaders, or bosses may decide. They can decide what they please, but you have your own purposes and the power to carry those purposes through. Thank you that I can have peace in my heart because you are in control. Please help me not to attempt to take on responsibilities that are not mine, and to trust you to help me with responsibilities that you give me. I do trust you, but I want to trust you more. Please help me.

I ask these things in your name. Amen.

15. ROOM

"And she gave birth to her firstborn son and wrapped him in swaddling cloths and laid him in a manger, because there was no place for them in the inn." (Luke 2:7)

We've all seen depictions of the Nativity scene. Some churches even have live scenes with animals crowding round the crib.

In all likelihood, though, there weren't any animals around the cradle of Jesus. They would have been out in the fields. We *are* told, however, that he was laid in a manger, which is a feeding trough used to feed cattle.

That doesn't mean that Jesus and Mary and the baby stayed in a barn. In all probability, Jesus was born in a cave right outside a home or outside an inn where sometimes animals were kept for shelter from the elements.

In this cave there probably would have been a little shelf hollowed out in the rock that could be used to put in foodstuffs to feed the livestock. That hollowed-out shelf was the manger.

So this is what we can picture: Joseph and Mary can't get into an inn. There's no hotel room available for them, no private residence in which to dwell, and so they seek shelter in a small cave. Perhaps there was straw on the floor and maybe the smell of animals in the air. The promised King of Israel is born not only in a small and insignificant town but in one of the most humble places in that town.

These circumstances of Jesus' birth call attention to something that marks the whole character of his life and ministry. When theologians examine the life of Christ, they notice that there is a basic progression in his lifetime: he moves from humiliation to exaltation.

Humiliation came first; it went from the humble circumstances of his birth, through his earthly ministry to the ignominy of his trial and of his rejection by his people, and, of course, the depths of humiliation which took place on the cross. Then glory burst through with his resurrection and then his ascension to heaven when he went to sit at the right hand of his Father.

This progress from humiliation to exaltation is not one that is absolutely steady. It's not the case that, throughout his earthly life, Jesus is totally shrouded and concealed in humiliation. The most notable example of this is at the Mount of Transfiguration, where, suddenly and without warning, as the disciples looked at Jesus, they saw that his face had begun to radiate light and his clothes had been transformed to become as bright as lightning (Luke 9:29). They fell on their faces in fear. It was his glory breaking through.

What is often overlooked is that this combination of humiliation and exaltation was evident right from the beginning. Even though Christ entered this world in circumstances of oppression and poverty—even though he arrived virtually incognito and was born in a shelter for animals and laid in a manger—yet, a very short distance away, there was an explosion of glory.

It came to the shepherds on the hillside:

> "An angel of the Lord appeared to them, and
> the glory of the Lord shone around them, and
> they were filled with great fear." (Luke 2:9)

The dazzling, blinding brightness of God's glory broke out and terrified these lowly shepherds. They had no idea of what was going on. They saw a blinding light that is associated with the throne of God himself, and then they heard the voice of the angel announcing the birth of their Savior: "For unto you is born this day in the city of David a Savior, who is Christ the Lord" (v 11).

Here was the King, the promised Messiah, the Son of David, come at last.

I wonder what the shepherds thought when they heard the angel's next words:

> "And this will be a sign for you: you will find a
> baby wrapped in swaddling cloths and lying in
> a manger." (v 12)

Lying in a manger? The Son of David had come. Yet even in the city of David, there was no room for him.

How will you praise this King of glory and humiliation today?

A PRAYER FOR TODAY

by Tim Challies

Father, we are so deeply challenged by the humility of Jesus. Though he is the God who created the world, he was willing to be born into the world. Though he is infinite and eternal, he was willing to enter into a specific time and place. Though he is immortal, he was willing to lay down his life. And all of this for the good of his people and your glory. It is only fitting, then, that you would highly exalt him and give him the name that is above every name. So even now, as we bow before him and confess his name, we ask that we would be willing and eager to imitate him in his humility. We pray that we would esteem others more highly than ourselves and count it all joy as we follow in the humble footsteps of our humble Savior.

Amen.

16. EMPTY

It was not just in the manger or on the light-filled hillside that glory and humiliation mingled in this story.

It's customary at Christmas to speak about the depths of the humiliation of Jesus' birth: the poor circumstances and the fact that he was born incognito to peasants. We stress the humiliation and the poverty into which Jesus was born. In other words, we tend to focus on what Jesus came to. We almost never examine the question of where Jesus came *from*.

Jesus answered that question when he said, "No one has ascended into heaven except he who descended from heaven" (John 3:13). The truth is, Jesus did not come from Bethlehem. He did not come from Nazareth. It was out of heaven that he came: out of the "ivory palaces," as Henry Barraclough's hymn puts it. "Out of the ivory palaces, into a world of woe."

I met Henry Barraclough unexpectedly once on a cold winter's night in Philadelphia. I asked him what inspired him to write that hymn, and he told me that he wrote it as a young man in 1915, after hearing a sermon on Philippians 2:6-8.

> "[Jesus], though he was in the form of God,
> did not count equality with God a thing to be
> grasped, but emptied himself, by taking the
> form of a servant, being born in the likeness
> of men. And being found in human form, he
> humbled himself by becoming obedient to the
> point of death, even death on a cross."

In Mr. Barraclough's time there was a debate raging about the meaning of this text. It was called the Kenosis Controversy. *Kenosis* is the Greek word for "emptying." Certain theologians were teaching the idea that when Philippians 2 says Jesus "emptied himself," it means he emptied himself of his deity. They claimed that he laid aside his divine attributes entirely, so that while Jesus of Nazareth was walking on the earth, he was a man and only a man.

The great theologian Benjamin Warfield responded to that by saying that the only *kenosis* that this demonstrated was the *kenosis* of the brains of the liberal theologians who were espousing it, because they would have to empty their minds of intelligence to seriously postulate the idea that God could, for even a second, stop being God.

Do you see his point? For God to lay aside his divine attributes would be impossible. The eternal, self-existent, unchanging God could not undergo an alteration. If God emptied himself of his Godness, the universe would be emptied of its existence, for it is in him that we live and move and have our being (Acts 17:28).

So if Jesus did not lay aside his deity, what did he empty himself of?

It wasn't his divine nature. It wasn't his omniscience. It wasn't his omnipotence. It wasn't any of those attributes of God that he laid aside. When Jesus emptied himself, he chose to take on our humanity, to not use his divine glory and privilege and prerogatives to advantage himself but to serve others.

Nobody took away Jesus' glory. Nobody stripped him of his privilege. Nobody ripped apart his status. He voluntarily took upon himself the role of the servant. And not just any old servant but a servant who would die for those he served.

Where did Jesus come *from*? Henry Barraclough heard the answer to this question that day in 1915. "As soon as I came back from that service," he told me, "I picked up my pen, and I began to write." He contemplated the emptying that our Savior did for us, and he penned the following words.

Out of the ivory palaces
Into a world of woe,
Only his great eternal love
Made my Savior go.

In what ways do you—or those around you—need to
know that great eternal love today?

A PRAYER FOR TODAY

by Steven J. Lawson

God, it is so hard for us to wrap our minds around the incarnation of Jesus Christ. How can we grasp that Jesus, as eternal God, took upon himself sinless humanity? But we believe it is true. It is hard for us to comprehend how Jesus is truly God, yet truly man. But we confess that it is so. We are deeply humbled by his humility. May his example produce lowliness of mind in us. We need to have the same attitude in us that was in Christ Jesus. We confess that we have not humbled ourselves enough or assumed the role of a servant to others. Forgive us for when we consider our own interests above the needs of others. Forgive us for when we desire to be served rather than to serve. Make us more like our Savior, who took upon himself the role of a servant and laid down his life for us.

We pray this in Jesus' name. Amen.

17. GLORY

Out of love, at the first Christmas, God the Son veiled his glory to be born as a baby—but, as we've seen already, that doesn't mean there wasn't glory to be found in his life on earth.

We've read about Mary and Joseph: the encounters with angels, the fearful journey to Bethlehem, the gloomy cave with its humble manger. From verse 8 of chapter 2—as we began to see a few chapters ago—Luke gives us a new point of view on the events of the first Christmas.

> "There were shepherds out in the field, keeping watch over their flock by night. And an angel of the Lord appeared to them, and the glory of the Lord shone around them, and they were filled with great fear." (Luke 2:8-9)

The old King James Version says, "And they were sore afraid." Newer translations have changed that because we don't speak that way anymore; we'd never say that somebody is "sore afraid." But I like it. It's one thing to be "afraid"; it's another thing to be "sore afraid." I guess that what the original translators were trying to get at was that these men were so afraid, it hurt. It was a fear that caused pain—because they were not accustomed to watching, with eyes unveiled, the visible manifestation of the glory of God.

You know how bright the sun can be. When a solar eclipse is about to take place, there are multiple warnings in the media. "You may be interested in this eclipse, but don't even for a second look directly into the core of the sun because such a view can do permanent damage to your eyes." The sun is too bright for our eyes to behold directly.

Yet the Scripture tells us that when the glory of God shines round about, it shines with a brightness that eclipses the sun (for example, Acts 26:13). If we cannot bear to look directly into the rays of the sun, which is merely a work of God's hands, how much less are we able to look directly into the unveiled presence of God's own shining glory. He's a consuming fire. He's too glorious and holy for any mortal to look at.

And here were the shepherds. Shepherds were men of such poor reputation that they were not allowed to bear witness in a courtroom in Israel—they were seen as untrustworthy. But it was to them, to the dregs of society, as they cared for their sheep in the darkness of the night, that instantly the sky was ablaze. It was not the sun, not the moon, not the stars, but the glory of God. Glory shone around them, and they were dazzled—terrified.

With the light came sound. With the manifestation of the glory of God came the utterance of the word of God through his messenger.

> "And the angel said to them, 'Fear not, for
> behold, I bring you good news of great joy that
> will be for all the people. For unto you is born
> this day in the city of David a Savior, who is
> Christ the Lord.'" (Luke 2:10-11)

"Fear not," the angel said. Why not? Because this was a time of unprecedented joy. This was the moment the world had been waiting for, and the shepherds had been selected to be spectators of it.

Jesus left heaven and veiled his glory—and why? So that we can be in glory with him one day. So that we can share glory with him. So that we can look into the face of God and not be afraid.

The angel said to the shepherds, *Today in the city of David a Savior has been born to you.* The Savior had been born—the glory had come—for *us.*

What difference can it make to you today to look forward to sharing God's glory?

A PRAYER FOR TODAY

by Joni Eareckson Tada

Heavenly Father, I don't think I will ever be able to wrap my heart, or my head, around your glory. You, in all your dazzling perfection, are reflected in Jesus, the perfect mirror image of yourself. O Father, no wonder you adore your Son—he is the photo image of all your beauty and excellence, mercy and might. No wonder you're enthralled with him! And Jesus, thank you for veiling your majesty to go through the great indignity of human birth. Though it meant humiliation and suffering, you and the Father agreed to this—all so that you would win yourself an eternal chorus of worshipers. An army of overcomers. And a radiant Bride with whom you will share your glory and on whom you will shower your love for all of eternity. I can hardly believe that that's me and my destiny. Oh, what a Christmas gift! Thank you, Jesus.

Amen.

18. ANGEL

Here is something extraordinary that we sometimes overlook about the New Testament and its teaching: the noun "angel" occurs more often in the New Testament than the noun "love." So—just in terms of frequency—we can say that the New Testament speaks more about angels than it does about love. I find that extremely interesting.

The word "angel" is used to describe created spirit beings that minister in the immediate presence of God. We see them in Isaiah 6, for example, around the throne of God, crying out, "Holy, holy, holy is the LORD of hosts" (v 3).

Most of the time when we read about angels, they are performing a specific function—one that is important to biblical history. Angels bring messages. God sends angels to Hagar (Genesis 16:7), Abraham (22:11), and

Jacob (31:11). An angel of the Lord gets in the way of Balaam to stop him sinning (Numbers 22:22-35) and appears to Gideon to spur him on to save Israel (Judges 6:11-24). Many times, when the Lord wants to do something in the life of his people, he sends an angel with a message.

It's no surprise that he does the same when it comes to the advent of Christ.

We know that before Jesus was born, his birth was first announced by an angel. The angel Gabriel came to Zechariah and talked about the birth of John the Baptist; that same angel Gabriel came to Mary and announced to her that she was going to have a baby. An angel appeared to Joseph in a dream. A multitude of angels appeared to the shepherds in the field outside Bethlehem, declaring the birth of Jesus. Angels feature heavily in the Christmas story.

But the point is never the angels themselves. It's always the message they bring.

"Behold," said the angel to the shepherds, "I bring you good news of great joy that will be for all the people" (Luke 2:10). *Good news,* is their message. The Greek word for good news is *euangelion*, and it's a word worth pausing over.

It begins with two letters, *eu*, which serve here as a prefix. You can perhaps think of some other words that start with the letters *eu*. A euphemism, for example—

that's a nice way of describing something that's not necessarily very pleasant. It's like going to the dentist and sitting in the dentist's chair and he says to you, "Now this may cause you a little discomfort." What is he really saying to you? "This is going to hurt, and it might hurt like crazy." He's using a euphemism: a good way of describing something that's basically bad or unpleasant.

Perhaps you know the word "euphonious." Something that is euphonious sounds good. Or what about a eulogy? A eulogy is a speech at a funeral, where someone stands up and gives some good words about the deceased person.

So we see that this little prefix *eu* simply means "good;" but the type of good in the word *euangelion* is not like that in "euphemism" or "eulogy." At the dentist's, "good" words may mask something bad. But when it comes to the Bible, *euangelion* is a good word that reveals something even better.

The main part of the word, *angelion*, means "message" or "announcement" or simply "news." This is from where we get the word "angel." An angel is a messenger—a bringer of news.

To Hagar, the angel brought the good news that the Lord had seen her and had a plan for her (Genesis 16:7-13). To Abraham, the angel brought the good news that he didn't have to kill his son (22:10-14). To Gideon, the angel brought the good news that God was with him and would save Israel through him (Judges 6:12, 14).

But to Mary, to Joseph, to Zechariah, and to the shepherds, the angels brought the best news of all—the supremely good news: the announcement of the coming of the Redeemer into the world.

God sent angels because he wanted people to know: this is *good* news.

Could you remind or tell someone else of this good news today?

A PRAYER FOR TODAY

by Sinclair B. Ferguson

*Lord Jesus Christ, our King, how great and
glorious yet how kind and loving you are! I thank
you today that you reign not only over sinners
whom you have redeemed but also over angels and
archangels, cherubim and seraphim who have
never needed redemption. How marvellous that
your Father sent heavenly messengers to announce
the good news of your coming to Mary and Joseph
and to the shepherds in the Bethlehem fields!
Lord, your word tells us that angels wonder what
it is like for us to experience your saving grace.
We deserve rejection, and yet you have loved us so
much. Help me to wonder with the angels and,
like them, to praise you. And help me also to find
their message about your love so amazing that, like
them, I will tell others about you.*

I ask this in your name. Amen.

19. HOST

"And suddenly," we read, "there was with the angel a multitude of the heavenly host" (Luke 2:13).

It brings to my mind an experience that took place in the Old Testament in the story of Elisha. There was a Syrian king who was trying to defeat the king of Israel, but every time he put together his battle plan and set up an ambush for the Israelites, the Israelites would avoid it. The king became convinced that there was a spy in his camp—or how else would the Israelites get wind of his plans? He summoned all his intelligence agents and asked who the spy was (2 Kings 6:8-11).

They reported, "None, my lord" (v 12). No, there was no spy in their midst. The problem, they explained, was Elisha the prophet. Everything that the Syrian king decided in secret to do, Elisha knew—because God told him.

It was Elisha who kept on warning the king of Israel. It was clear that the only way the Syrians would beat the Israelites was if they got rid of Elisha.

So the Syrian king sent an army in the middle of the night to Dothan, the city where Elijah was living. "He sent there horses and chariots and a great army, and they came by night and surrounded the city" (v 14). Then they waited.

Morning dawned, and Elisha's servant got up and went outside. What did he see but numerous chariots of the enemy surrounding them? He looked to the east, he looked to the west, he looked to the north, he looked to the south—and everywhere he looked, there were soldiers and chariots. The servant was terrified, and he ran and said to Elisha, "Alas, my master! What shall we do?" (v 15). And he presumably told Elisha that they were surrounded by enemy soldiers.

Elisha looked at his servant and said, "Do not be afraid, for those who are with us are more than those who are with them" (v 16).

Elisha's servant was most likely wondering, *Is Elisha out of his mind?* I imagine he looked out of the windows and started counting the enemy chariots. There were thousands of soldiers, but on Elisha's side, there were only the two of them. What could the prophet mean?

Elisha prayed and said, "O Lord, please open his eyes that he may see." Then the narrative goes on:

"So the Lord opened the eyes of the young man,
and he saw, and behold, the mountain was full
of horses and chariots of fire all around Elisha."

(v 17)

What that servant was privileged to see was the heavenly host.

God has an invisible army of angels—and it's that same army that came to Bethlehem. Luke tells us that while the first angel was speaking to the shepherds, suddenly there appeared "a multitude of the heavenly host": that is, a multitude of the heavenly army. But on this occasion they weren't there to fight and to protect a prophet in danger. They were there to celebrate the good news.

What a show. First the light and then the sound—the sound of an army of angels singing an anthem of praise.

"Glory to God in the highest, and on earth
peace." (Luke 2:14)

How can you join in with the angels' song?

A PRAYER FOR TODAY

by Chris Larson

*Our Father and our God, we join with the angels
in praising you, singing with joyful hearts that
the Lord has come. We sing, "Glory to God in the
highest" for the peace you have brought to those
upon whom your favor rests. Lord, we confess we
are born blind to your glory, but we testify that
your Spirit opens the eyes of our natural heart
so that we may perceive that which is spiritual.
May we trust you today. May we live with an
awareness of your presence all our days. You have
said that you will never leave us or forsake us;
help us to face the perils and sadnesses of this
life knowing that you are powerfully present. We
rejoice that Christ has come and that Christ will
come again, bringing your justice upon the world
and your people to their heavenly home, where
we will be in the company of countless angels,
worshiping for eternity.*

Amen.

20. GO

"The shepherds said to one another, 'Let us go over to Bethlehem and see this thing that has happened.' " (Luke 2:15)

These shepherds had been overwhelmed by the blazing, dazzling light of divine glory, and their ears had heard the announcement of the messengers of God that their Savior had been born. The angel had told them that they would find a sign: a sign that would confirm to them the fulfillment of their deepest expectations, their wildest dreams, and their most moving hopes.

"You will find a baby wrapped in swaddling cloths and lying in a manger." (v 12)

The shepherds didn't wait another minute. One of them looked at the others and said, "Let us go." *Let's not wait till morning. Let's not wait for ten minutes. I want to go there right now.* It's one of my favourite parts in the whole of Scripture. *Let us go.* There's something about that one line that has always grabbed me. After they heard this announcement and saw this blinding light, they looked at one another and said, "Let us go."

They went with haste (v 16), and they found him. They saw the reason for this breakthrough of heavenly glory—this heavenly sound-and-light show. They found the baby lying in a manger wrapped in swaddling clothes.

If you knew that God was present a short distance from where you are at this moment, how long would you wait before you went to see him? Two thousand years have passed since the shepherds said, "Let us go" and made haste to find him—and yet there are still people who are in no hurry whatsoever to go and look for Jesus.

It is particularly tragic when we see the same pattern of behavior emerging even among Christians. Multitudes start the Christian life with a brief flare that fizzles out. They learn a few Bible verses, make a cursory reading of the New Testament, take a crash course in evangelism, learn a few perfunctory prayers, and then level off on a plateau of stagnated growth.

Yet God calls his people to much more. Christ calls his disciples to go—and not just to go to him but to go into the whole world.

"All authority in heaven and on earth has been given to me. Go therefore and make disciples of all nations, baptizing them in the name of the Father and of the Son and of the Holy Spirit, teaching them to observe all that I have commanded you. And behold, I am with you always, to the end of the age."

(Matthew 28:18-20)

We are to share the gospel with everyone so that more and more people might call Jesus "Master." This calling is not simply a call to evangelism. It isn't merely a call to get members for our churches. Rather, Christ calls us to make disciples. Disciples are people who have wholeheartedly committed to following the thinking and conduct of the Master. Such discipleship is a lifelong experience of learning the mind of Christ and following the will of Christ, submitting ourselves in full obedience to his lordship.

We need to be ready to go. We should long to be those who want to learn, to grow, and to develop in our personal understanding of Christ and of the things of God. Christians are to be people who are serious about our faith and want it to be fully developed; people who go into all the world with Christ's agenda, not our own, in order to produce more disciples—to flood the world with knowledgeable, articulate Christians who worship God and follow Jesus Christ passionately.

That's my prayer for you in this Christmas season—that you will go now and look for the one who was born for you: Christ the Lord. That you will know his love more deeply and fully, and comprehend its breadth and length and depth, and help others to do the same, day after day.

What is one way in which you could seek Jesus more fully?

A PRAYER FOR TODAY

by Rosemary Jensen

Dear Lord Jesus, I love to sing, "Christ for the world we sing; the world to Christ we bring,"* because you want me to be one of those who bring Christ to the world. I know that by myself I can't reach the whole world, but by your grace I can reach at least a small part of my world. I pray that during this Christmas season, you will fill me with your Spirit to tell those you want to save about you—that you are the way, the truth, and the life. I have missed so many opportunities to talk about you, and I ask you to forgive me. I now ask you to help me not miss a single opportunity this Christmas to tell others about you. If you are calling me to reach out to more than my family and neighbors, please show me where you want me to go.

I ask this in your precious name. Amen.

* *"Christ for the World We Sing" by Samuel Wolcott*

21. HOLY

"And when the time came for their purification
according to the Law of Moses, they brought
him up to Jerusalem to present him to the
Lord (as it is written in the Law of the Lord,
'Every male who first opens the womb shall be
called holy to the Lord') and to offer a sacrifice
according to what is said in the Law of the Lord,
'a pair of turtledoves, or two young pigeons.'"

(Luke 2:22-24)

Mary and Joseph made the trip to the temple
for two reasons. First, they came to dedicate
their firstborn child to the service of God. That was a
traditional custom in Israel. Luke is referring here to
several Old Testament texts which said that the first
male child to come from the womb was to be regarded

as holy—he was set apart, sacred, consecrated to God (Exodus 13:12-13; 34:19-20; Numbers 18:15).

Most Christians, when they hear the term "holy," think of righteousness and ethical purity. After all, God's word in many passages associates holiness with righteous living and being cleansed from sin (for example 2 Corinthians 7:1; 1 Peter 1:14-16). Nevertheless, although holiness in Scripture is associated with moral uprightness, it is not chiefly about doing the right things. To be holy is, first and foremost, to be set apart from what is common. It is to be different in contrast to the world. Something or someone is made holy when the Almighty, who is himself set apart from all creation, sets it apart for a special use or purpose.

This Jewish practice of setting apart the firstborn child of any family pointed to the fact that God had set apart an entire people for himself.

It was a reminder of how God had saved his people at the first Passover. The Israelites were enslaved in Egypt, and God provided a way for them to escape. They were required to mark the lintels and doorposts of their homes with the blood of lambs (Exodus 12:21-28). It set their homes apart from those of the Egyptians.

The angel of death went throughout the land on that night and killed the firstborn in every family who had not marked their doorposts. And so, in each household there was a death: either of a lamb or of a child.

God certainly did not need the bloody marking on the doorposts to tell his people apart from the Egyptians. The need for the sign points to a deeper theological reality. Judgment would be passing through the land indiscriminately; every family was subject to the punishment that would be meted out, even the Israelites. There was nothing inherent in them that made them any less deserving of death than their Egyptian oppressors. But marking the door with blood signified that death had already taken place in that household—judgment had been meted out there, albeit on a substitute victim. The angel of death would thus pass over that home without inflicting harm (v 23).

It was a sign to the Israelites that they too were sinners deserving of death—yet they had a way to escape destruction. They were set apart from the Egyptians and allowed to escape, not because of anything they had done but by God's grace.

After that, a sacrifice had to be made for every firstborn son, just as at that first Passover. It was a reminder that the Israelites were a people set apart—a people rescued by the Lord's hand (Exodus 13:14-16).

The second reason why Mary and Joseph came to the temple was that in addition to this ceremony of dedication, they also performed the rite of purification. This involved the offering of sacrifices: a burnt offering and a sin offering. This pointed to our corporate fallenness as human beings. An offering had to be made to atone for sin, even for a tiny baby. Once again, in this practice we see God's grace. By nature humans are not holy. We are sinful and fallen, far away from God's glory, power, and purity. Yet he makes a way for our sin to be atoned for and for us to come close to Him. He sets us apart and makes us holy.

In this way, the events of the first Christmas begin to point us forward to the events of the first Easter. For in this scene, we watch Joseph and Mary come to the temple for the rites of purification and dedication, in obedience to the Old Testament law. We see them present their firstborn to the Lord. And we know what they do not yet realize: that he himself will one day be the perfect and final atoning sacrifice for sin.

In what ways are you aware of your fallenness today? How can you celebrate Jesus' atoning sacrifice and the holiness he has given to you?

A PRAYER FOR TODAY

by Tim Challies

Our Father, we profess what you so often declare about yourself—that you are holy, holy, holy. And at the same time we admit what you so often tell us about ourselves—that we are not holy. We confess that we have fallen from the state in which you created us. We confess this and ask your forgiveness. We hear your promise that if we confess our sins, you are faithful and just to forgive us our sins and to cleanse us from all unrighteousness. So we joyfully, humbly receive your forgiveness— forgiveness earned by your Son, our Savior. And now we ask that by your Spirit you would enable us to live lives of true holiness. Let us live before you as those who have been made holy, who have been set apart, who have been given the glorious calling to live for you and for your glory.

Amen.

22. WAITING

"Now there was a man in Jerusalem, whose
name was Simeon, and this man was righteous
and devout, waiting for the consolation of
Israel, and the Holy Spirit was upon him."

(Luke 2:25)

Simeon was an old man. Some time before—we don't
know how long—he had received a message from
God the Holy Spirit about the coming of the Messiah.
We've seen a number of these messages already; repeatedly
in the Old Testament, the Spirit of God came upon the
prophets, and they announced the future coming of Jesus.
But the message Simeon received was unlike the other divine revelations concerning the coming of the Messiah.

Simeon was selected by God to receive a unique promise. God told him that he would not die until he saw the
promised Christ (v 26).

There have been many false prophets who have made that kind of promise through the years—and many people who have been sorely disappointed. I remember being in San Francisco once and seeing a large mass of people assembled by the side of a cliff. I asked the people who were hosting me what all those people were doing. "Oh," they said, "they're part of a group of people who received a prophecy that Jesus is coming back today, right here on this hillside."

All these people were gathered there in joyous expectation, waiting for the return of Christ, and when I came back down the hill later in the day, they were still there. The sun had set, the day had ended, and they were still waiting.

Many people have been deceived into thinking that the return of Jesus would be in their lifetime, and you can see why they are often ridiculed for their ungrounded hope. When I think about Simeon, I can't help but think of the torment that this man may have endured throughout his life. We don't know from the pages of Scripture whether Simeon ever told anybody during his life that he had received this revelation from God. But let's suppose for a minute that he did. What would have been the reaction of his friends and of his neighbors? They would have thought the man was not of sound mind.

It's easy to imagine people in the temple wagging their heads and whispering behind his back: *There's that silly old man. He comes here every single day. He thinks he's not going to die until he sees the Messiah. Poor thing.* Perhaps tour guides would lead the crowds through the streets of Jerusalem—*Over here is the temple, and on your right is the fortress*—and as they came into the temple courts they would add, *And over here is an old man, the Fool of Jerusalem, who comes here every day looking for the Messiah.*

And then the day came.

> "[Simeon] came in the Spirit into the temple,
> and when the parents brought in the child
> Jesus, to do for him according to the custom
> of the Law, he took him up in his arms and
> blessed God." (v 27-28)

Think of it: how many times, through how many years, had this man waited and searched and longed to see the Messiah? Then one day, when his eyes were dim and he had grown old, he entered the temple and saw Mary and Joseph and the baby. How many thousands of babies had he already seen? But when he looked at this baby, instantly he knew: this was the Christ child. God had kept his promise and sent his Son.

Simeon's life may have seemed foolish, but it turned out to have been well spent. It was a life grounded in faith in the promises of God—and that can never be a waste.

And so at last the old man took the child in his arms.

Do you ever worry about appearing foolish because of your faith? How does Simeon's example help you?

A PRAYER FOR TODAY

by Steven J. Lawson

God, it is challenging for us to wait on your timetable. We grow so easily impatient and weary; we want everything to fall into place immediately. But we know that you have an appointed time for everything under the sun. Grant to us patience so that we can learn to trust your purposes. We ask that you would increase our endurance so that we can bear up under the pressure that we are facing at this present moment. Help us to be steadfast as we wait for you to bring to pass your plans. Forgive us for being impetuous and wanting a quick resolution to our problems. While others around us are jumping to act upon their own solutions, grant us the patience to wait for your abundant provisions to come in your perfect timing. In the meantime, help us to rest in you.

We pray this in Jesus' name. Amen.

23. FACE-TO-FACE

There's a stage in life when you're not old enough yet to retire, but you are old enough for people to start talking to you about retirement. "Do you have a retirement program?" they start to ask. "Do you have a retirement nest egg? Do you have a retirement (fill in the blank)?"

When people say those things to me, I look at them and say, "What do you mean, retire?" A person doesn't retire from the work of God. You may change the direction of your labor, but you don't ever, ever stop seeking to be faithful to God.

I had a friend who was a missionary. He was in his eighties, he was infirm, and he couldn't do any physical work anymore. But he said to me, "I can still labor eight hours a day." I asked him, "What do you do?" He said, "I pray. That's all I can do." He wasn't retired.

While we're alive, we don't retire from the work of God, but we do long for the day when we can retire into our final rest—when we can behold Jesus face to face, just as Simeon did.

Simeon was waiting for "the consolation of Israel," Luke 2:25 tells us, and that's what Jesus was. He came to a nation of people in need of consolation: a people who had known and endured relentless years of suffering and of want. The prophet Jeremiah, who saw his people go into slavery and exile, cried out, "Is there no balm in Gilead? Is there no physician there?" (Jeremiah 8:22). That is, *can there be no healing for the people of God?* The promised land was supposed to be a place of rest and plenty (Joshua 21:44-45), but things seemed to have gone wrong. Now the nation of Israel needed a new rest. They needed healing, comfort, consolation—and they knew that all that was to be embodied in the Messiah.

Simeon looked into Jesus' face.

What would it mean to you to look visibly into the face of Christ? Let me remind you that God in his spiritual, invisible nature does not have a face. The only face that he has is the face that he wore in the incarnation. That's what we celebrate at Christmas: not simply the birth of a baby but the incarnation of God himself, God with us, the God whose face can be seen. Here is "the image of the invisible God" (Colossians 1:15).

I think of the many scenes in the New Testament

where people beheld him face to face. I think of those who looked into the tortured, twisted face of Christ as he was making atonement for our sins on the cross. I think of the women who came to the tomb seeking the body of Christ: how they were so distressed when they couldn't find it, and how they looked into the face of a man whom they thought at first was the gardener. I think of those who saw his face at the ascension, as he was lifted up into the clouds.

But as magnificent as all of those events were, none exceeded in glory the single glance of Simeon into the face of this baby. He said:

> "Lord, now you are letting your servant depart
>   in peace,
>   according to your word;
>   for my eyes have seen your salvation
>   that you have prepared in the presence of
>   all peoples,
>   a light for revelation to the Gentiles,
>   and for glory to your people Israel."
>
> (Luke 2:29-32)

Simeon saw and recognized the consolation of Israel, and it was enough. Now he could rest.

And so can you and I, one day. Today we see "in a mirror dimly," but one day we will see Jesus face to face (1 Corinthians 13:12). We will see what Simeon saw, and we will fully rest. Until then, our hearts can find rest in the knowledge that that day is coming. We don't retire. There's labor to be done for the Lord—and this labor is not in vain (1 Corinthians 15:58).

How do you think you will respond when you see Jesus face to face?

A PRAYER FOR TODAY

by Joni Eareckson Tada

Lord Jesus, on that day, among the countless billions, I think you will look for me. You will have a special kindness for me and a particular grace. And in that breathless moment when I see you face to face, I may collapse to my knees, stunned with the brilliant newness of being glorified. In that moment, let me gaze up at you, reach for your hand, and say, "Thank you, Jesus, for dying for me." And you will know I mean it, for you'll recognize me as the one who came to you in constant need of grace, hemorrhaging human strength, morning, noon, and night. Help me to press on toward the high goal of this calling, never taking it for granted but seizing the days that draw me closer and closer to you.

In your matchless name, amen.

24. PEOPLE

Why did Jesus do it? Why was he willing to give up his glory?

A simple answer is to say, "God so loved the world, that he gave his only Son, that whoever believes in him should not perish but have eternal life" (John 3:16). Every Christian knows that the Bible teaches that. Everybody knows that God loves the world, and that behind all of this drama of redemption stands the incredible love of God.

But that doesn't quite explain Jesus' prayer to his Father in John 17, at the other end of his life on earth—on the night before he died.

> "I have manifested your name to the people
> whom you gave me out of the world. Yours
> they were, and you gave them to me, and they
> have kept your word." (v 6)

> "I am praying for them. I am not praying for
> the world but for those whom you have given
> me, for they are yours." (v 9)

Why did Jesus come? Because of his great, arresting, gripping, abiding love for his sheep: for all those whom the Father had given him. Because of his unbelievable love for the church. Yes, there's a sense in which God loves the whole world. But there is a special sense in which God loves his people.

Jesus stripped himself of his dignity and his glory. He came to this planet, into this world of woe, and he came under the authority of evil people who mocked him and judged him and ridiculed him. He was clothed with the sins of others, and he took our punishment.

He did it for the ones who had been chosen since the foundation of the world to belong to God.

Imagine the conversation that took place within the Godhead in eternity past. *Son, from the foundation of the world I have chosen my people. They are mine. They belong to me, and I'm giving them to you as a gift. And this is what you will do for them.*

This was not an indiscriminate blast with a redemptive shotgun. Jesus didn't come in the mere hope that someone would take up his offer of redemption. He had chosen who would be redeemed. God's purpose and plan from all eternity was to send Jesus Christ into the world for you and for me, if we are believers. Jesus understood that. And so he prayed:

> "I do not ask for these [the first disciples]
> only, but also for those who will believe in
> me through their word, that they may all be
> one, just as you, Father, are in me, and I in
> you, that they also may be in us, so that the
> world may believe that you have sent me. The
> glory that you have given me I have given to
> them, that they may be one even as we are
> one, I in them and you in me, that they may
> become perfectly one, so that the world may
> know that you sent me and loved them even
> as you loved me. Father, I desire that they
> also, whom you have given me, may be with
> me where I am, to see my glory that you have
> given me because you loved me before the
> foundation of the world." (v 20-24)

I can hardly believe what Jesus has done to ensure the redemption of his people—the definite and particular redemption of his sheep. In that first advent, he came to live a life of perfect obedience, he died for our transgressions, and he rose again. He prayed for us, and prays for us still. He prays that we may be one: all God's people, united as Jesus and the Father are united. He prays that we may be in him, united with the Father. He prays that one day we may be with him where he is, to see his glory, which God gave him because he loved him—even as he loved us—before the foundation of the world.

We, as his children, have dignity, status, privilege, honor, and glory. At his second advent, that glory will be made perfect.

> "Beloved, we are God's children now, and what we will be has not yet appeared; but we know that when he appears we shall be like him, because we shall see him as he is."
>
> (1 John 3:2)

How can you express your oneness with Christ and with his people this Christmas?

A PRAYER FOR TODAY

by Sinclair B. Ferguson

*Heavenly Father, I have tried too often to find
in myself the reason why you love me. I have
mistakenly thought it was because of what I have
been and done. But I see now that you have loved
me only because of your love for me, not mine for
you. I tremble when I remember that this love
stretches back to before creation—it is too much
to take in. Father, it moves me to know that I am
your love gift to the Lord Jesus. Please help me to
see how much I mean to him—because I mean
so much to you. Enable me to think of my fellow
Christians in this way too. Give us a Jesus-like love
for one another until, at last, we are together for
ever in his presence.*

*Hear me, Father, because I pray this in Jesus'
name. Amen.*

ABOUT THE PRAYER
CONTRIBUTORS

CHRIS LARSON is president and CEO at Ligonier, an international ministry founded by Dr R.C. Sproul to proclaim the holiness of God in all its fullness to as many people as possible. He previously worked in education and the corporate world.

ROSEMARY JENSEN is the founder and president of The Rafiki Foundation, a mission organization working in Africa, and The Rosemary Jensen Bible Foundation. She served as Executive Director of Bible Study Fellowship for many years.

TIM CHALLIES is a Christian blogger and author who worships and serves as an elder at Grace Fellowship Church in Toronto, Ontario. His website features book reviews, articles on the Christian life, and curated lists of recommended blogs and resources. He is the co-founder of Cruciform Press.

DR STEVEN J. LAWSON is founder and president of OnePassion Ministries in Dallas, Texas, a teaching fellow at Ligonier, and Professor of Preaching at The Master's Seminary. Having served as a pastor for over 40 years in Arkansas and Alabama, he is currently lead preacher at Trinity Bible Church of Dallas.

JONI EARECKSON TADA is CEO of Joni and Friends, an organization that provides help and support to special-needs families and equips churches in developing disability ministry. She is the author of numerous books, including *A Spectacle of Glory* and the children's book *The Awesome Super Fantastic Forever Party*.

DR SINCLAIR B. FERGUSON is Chancellor's Professor of Systematic Theology at Reformed Theological Seminary. A native of Scotland, he worships at Trinity Church, Aberdeen, where he also serves as the honorary associate preacher. He is a teaching fellow at Ligonier and the author of many books.

the good book

COMPANY

BIBLICAL | RELEVANT | ACCESSIBLE

At The Good Book Company, we are dedicated to helping Christians and local churches grow. We believe that God's growth process always starts with hearing clearly what he has said to us through his timeless word—the Bible.

Ever since we opened our doors in 1991, we have been striving to produce Bible-based resources that bring glory to God. We have grown to become an international provider of user-friendly resources to the Christian community, with believers of all backgrounds and denominations using our books, Bible studies, devotionals, evangelistic resources, and DVD-based courses.

We want to equip ordinary Christians to live for Christ day by day, and churches to grow in their knowledge of God, their love for one another, and the effectiveness of their outreach.

Call us for a discussion of your needs or visit one of our local websites for more information on the resources and services we provide.

Your friends at The Good Book Company

thegoodbook.com | thegoodbook.co.uk
thegoodbook.com.au | thegoodbook.co.nz
thegoodbook.co.in